Original title:
Pensive Paradoxes

Copyright © 2024 Creative Arts Management OÜ
All rights reserved.

Author: Eleanor Prescott
ISBN HARDBACK: 978-9916-90-708-5
ISBN PAPERBACK: 978-9916-90-709-2

The Beauty of Conflicting Dualities

In shadows dance the light of day,
Two paths diverge, both lead astray.
A whisper sings where thunder rolls,
Embracing peace while chaos tolls.

The sun embraces the coldest night,
Soft shadows linger at dawn's first light.
In every heart, a struggle waged,
Where love and fear are oft engaged.

In the Midst of Splintered Realities

Fragments scatter like leaves in flight,
Each piece a truth, a paradox bright.
In twisted streets, the lost souls roam,
Searching for warmth in a world, a home.

A mirror cracks, reflects a sigh,
Faces change as the seasons fly.
What is real among the dreams?
Life is stitched with fragile seams.

The Silence of Chaotic Thoughts

In the noise of a restless mind,
Thoughts collide, yet peace we find.
Amidst the turmoil, whispers glow,
A gentle pause, the inner flow.

Ideas crash like waves at sea,
In silence, chaos sets us free.
Moments linger, deeply fraught,
Yet clarity blooms from tangled thought.

Gazing at the Horizon of Doubt

Beyond the mist where shadows lie,
Questions flutter like birds in the sky.
Each step forward, a tethered glance,
Into the unknown, we take a chance.

The horizon stretches, a canvas gray,
Painted whispers mark the way.
In the cloak of uncertainty, we tread,
With hope as our compass, by dreams we are led.

When Dreams Clash

In shadows where hopes collide,
Whispers of wishes, time won't bide.
Fates entwined in a dance of doubt,
Echoes of laughter fade, then shout.

Stars collide in the midnight sky,
A symphony of 'what ifs' sigh.
Hearts diverge, yet yearn to meet,
Paths once clear now feel discreet.

The Edge of Knowing

At dawn's break, the truth does tease,
With flickers of light in the gentle breeze.
A world powerful yet so unclear,
On the brink of wisdom, we draw near.

Whispers echo from ages past,
Each lesson learned, forever cast.
To seek the answers, always bold,
The edge of knowing, stories told.

Confessions of a Wandering Soul

In alleys where the lost reside,
Stories murmur with every stride.
A heart that roams, forever free,
In search of places yet to see.

Beneath the stars, where dreams align,
Echoes of laughter, remnants of wine.
Each soul a chapter, a tale to share,
In this vast universe, none despair.

Tides of Yearning

Like waves that crash on restless shores,
Yearning redefines what longing implores.
A dance of hope, a pull of fate,
In the ocean of dreams, we anticipate.

Under moonlight, desires unfold,
Each whisper of winds, secrets told.
The heart, a compass, forever drawn,
To the horizon, where dawn is born.

The Paradox of Comfort

Wrapped in warmth, a soft embrace,
Yet shadows linger, filling space.
Familiar paths, they soothe the soul,
But bind us tight, they take their toll.

A whisper calls, to venture wide,
While comfort tugs to stay inside.
In stillness finds a silent fight,
The paradox of wrong and right.

Notes from a Half-formed Thought

Caught in limbo, ideas swim,
Glimmers of light on the edge of whim.
Words stumble forth, in fits and starts,
Fragments of dreams, and scattered parts.

A notion half-drawn, like fleeting mist,
Incomplete visions gently kissed.
They linger softly, a tender tease,
Awaiting form, a mind's release.

The Weight of Unanswered Whys

Questions heavy, hearts weigh down,
In silence drown, where thoughts can drown.
Each why a stone, bound to the soul,
A quest for truth, elusive goal.

The echoes ring in empty halls,
As reason fades, belief enthralls.
Chasing shadows, what lies ahead?
In search of answers left unsaid.

Footprints in Opposing Directions

Marks in sand, a tale they weave,
Journeys differ, we must believe.
Two paths diverge, both strong, distinct,
At every choice, where hearts are linked.

Yet here we stand, at last, unsure,
In every stride, what we endure.
Footprints trace life's tangled threads,
In opposing ways our love still spreads.

The Truth in the Tension

In shadows deep, where secrets dwell,
The heartbeats echo, a lover's swell.
Caught between halves, the push and pull,
In silence, our fears begin to lull.

Words left unspoken, weigh heavy on lips,
A dance in the dark, lost in the grips.
Navigating doubts, the night holds sway,
But truth finds a way to light the day.

Balancing on the Edge

A step on the brink, the world spins fast,
With courage held close, we breathe at last.
Between the abyss and sky so wide,
We waver, we dance, on this fragile tide.

The whispers of warning, a siren's call,
Yet freedom's thrill can conquer it all.
Each heartbeat a wager, so full of grace,
We balance our dreams in this daring space.

Enigmatic Whispers of Affection

Your eyes hold secrets, a universe vast,
In glances exchanged, we forge our path.
Like stars in the night, our souls intertwine,
With silence that speaks, a love so divine.

A touch like a breeze, a spark in the dark,
In the quietest moments, ignites the heart.
With every breath shared, a promise takes flight,
In enigmatic whispers, love finds its light.

The Weight of a Thousand Choices

Every road traveled, a lesson we learn,
With forks in the path, our passions will burn.
The weight of decisions, they cling like a shroud,
Yet every small step brings hope to the crowd.

In moments of doubt, we gather our strength,
With each little choice, we measure the length.
Together we journey, through joy and through pain,
The weight of our choices, our courage, our gain.

The Weight of Lightness

In the quiet hush of dawn,
Wings flutter with a gentle song.
Promises dance on the breeze,
Carrying dreams where hearts belong.

Laughter echoes through the air,
Footsteps of those who roam free.
Each moment hangs, a breath of joy,
That weighs nothing, yet feels like glee.

Sunbeams touch the morning dew,
Sparkling like crystals in flight.
An embrace of warmth surrounds,
Transforming shadows into light.

Together we drift, unbound,
In this world where time stands still.
The weight of lightness lifts our souls,
Guiding us with love's sweet will.

The Color of Unlived Moments

Brush strokes on an empty canvas,
Hues wait for stories untold.
Each shade a whisper of chances,
Fleeting dreams that could unfold.

Silent echoes, roads not taken,
Painted skies of missed delights.
In the heart, a longing lingers,
For vibrant days and starry nights.

Crimson sunsets, golden dawns,
Memories of life's sweet refrain.
Colors blend, yet fade away,
Leaving depths of wistful pain.

But in every breath, hope lies,
An open door to what can be.
Embrace the hues of possibility,
As life invites us to see.

Harmonies of the Unresolved

In the silence hums a question,
Notes suspended in the air.
Tension builds, a sweet uncertainty,
A melody that brings us where.

Fingers dance over the keys,
Searching for the perfect sound.
Each pause holds a breath of wonder,
In the music, truths abound.

Voices merge and intertwine,
Whispers of the unresolved.
In the space between the notes,
Resilience grows, mysteries solved.

Together we seek the rhythm,
The harmony in our fears.
For in the mix of doubt and hope,
We find the strength to draw near.

When Answers Become Questions

In the twilight of knowing,
Certainty begins to wane.
Searching eyes lose their focus,
As the familiar turns to strange.

What was clear now feels clouded,
Paths once straight begin to bend.
Every truth in shadows dances,
In the light where questions blend.

Chasing echoes through the corridors,
The heart finds wisdom in doubt.
For every answer opens doors,
To questions we can't live without.

Embrace the unsure and unclear,
In the mysteries of the mind.
For in the questions lies the beauty,
Of a journey one must find.

Dancing with Disquiet

In silence we sway, with doubts in our chest,
Steps pulled apart by the weight of unrest.
A rhythm unsteady, hearts beat out of time,
Chasing the whispers that tease and that chime.

Shadows move close, in the flickering light,
Each glance revealing a truth mid-flight.
The dance of the anxious, a nervous ballet,
We twirl in the chaos, then drift far away.

Footfalls echo in chambers of fear,
With every misstep, the way seems unclear.
Holding our breath as the music will pause,
Each silence a question, no need for applause.

Yet in the disturbance, a spark ignites,
Fining our courage in flickers and flights.
Through the disquiet, we learn to embrace,
The beauty that flourishes, hiding our grace.

The Complexity of Simple Truths

Truths often dressed in the guise of a lie,
Beneath the surface, the subtle will pry.
What seems so clear can be lost in the fog,
We seek out the light, but it hides like a dog.

A smile can mask the weight of despair,
A simple gesture can lay our hearts bare.
Questions emerge with an innocent face,
In the maze of this life, we wander and chase.

Simple as whispers, complex as a storm,
We clench onto meaning, our minds start to swarm.
In shadows of wisdom, our fears intertwine,
The pursuit of the truth can be bitter, benign.

Yet as we unravel the knots that we weave,
In the heart of confusion, we dare to believe.
Understanding grows in the cracks of the night,
In the search for the simple, we find our true light.

Paradox in a Wishing Well

They toss in their pennies, their wishes in tow,
In silence they ponder what fate may bestow.
Hope dances lightly on the edges of dreams,
While echoes of doubt swim in cold, starry streams.

The water reflects every longing and sigh,
Churning with secrets the heart can't deny.
Each wish is a whisper, a fleeting caress,
Yet cloaked in the paradox of want and excess.

What if the wish is the barrier we chase?
Constrained by our hopes, caught in a race.
The well, ever waiting, holds stories untold,
Of dreams left unspoken, of futures bold.

So cast in your wish, yet beware the embrace,
For longing may lead us to lost, empty space.
Yet amidst the chaos, a truth can still swell,
Beauty often blooms where the waters compel.

Amongst the Shadows of Certainty

In the still of the night, where questions reside,
Certainty casts its unrelenting guide.
Yet shadows emerge in the corners of thought,
Doubts form like whispers that linger, unrought.

Each path marked with claims of what's right and wrong,
Yet in tangled beliefs, we often feel strong.
Yet the shadows remind us with every bold stance,
That certainty's grip can complicate the dance.

We paint our convictions in brush strokes so bold,
Yet the heart holds a truth seldom seen or told.
In the grip of the known, the unknown runs deep,
Awakening echoes that stir us from sleep.

To wander through shadows, to question, explore,
In the fabric of certainty lies so much more.
Embrace the ambiguity, let doubt lead the way,
For midst the shadows, new find light of day.

Silent Echoes of a Turbulent Heart

In the shadows where whispers dwell,
Lost secrets weave a silent spell.
A heart that beats with trembling might,
Echoes softly through the night.

Upon the waves of restless seas,
Thoughts collide like autumn leaves.
Turbulence in every sigh,
As dreams and fears begin to fly.

Veins of stormy winds entwine,
In the stillness, pain does rhyme.
Yet in the chaos, light will gleam,
A fragile hope within the dream.

With each heartbeat, stories fade,
Silent echoes of love betrayed.
Yet through the dark, a spark takes flight,
Crafting solace from the night.

Surreal Crossroads

Underneath an azure sky,
Where shadowed paths intersect nigh.
Reality bends, time unwinds,
Mysteries swirl in wandering minds.

Footsteps dance on cobblestone,
In this realm, we are not alone.
Choices whisper with gentle grace,
In surreal worlds, we find our place.

Illusions bloom in vibrant hues,
Each forked road offers hidden clues.
With every glance, a dream ignites,
Guiding souls through enchanted nights.

At the junction, heartbeats race,
Navigating time and space.
Embracing fate's peculiar art,
We weave our dreams, a work of heart.

The Unraveling Thread

Stitch by stitch, the pattern frays,
Whispers of time in frayed displays.
Each moment holds a subtle thread,
Binding stories left unsaid.

A tapestry of joy and strife,
Woven tightly, breath of life.
Yet fingers tremble as they tug,
On threads that bind the heart with grief.

Frayed edges of what once was whole,
Symbols of love, a fractured soul.
Yet in the mess, beauty finds rest,
In tangled paths, we are blessed.

With gentle hands, we start anew,
Embracing every shade and hue.
In each unraveling, strength we see,
The thread of life, wild and free.

Within the Embrace of Dissonance

In a world of clashing sound,
Harmony lost, chaos found.
Yet in the clash, a song can rise,
Beauty hidden from our eyes.

Melodies dance with jarring notes,
In a sea where stillness floats.
The heartbeats pound, a wild race,
Finding rhythm in displace.

With every tear, a note is played,
In dissonance, we are remade.
The discord sings, a clarion call,
Within the chaos, we find our all.

Embrace the noise, let feelings soar,
In the fractures, we are more.
For even in the storm's advance,
We can thrive within each chance.

A Canvas of Contradiction

In shadows dance the vibrant hues,
A clash of silence, loud as news.
Joy in sorrow, light in dark,
A puzzle whispered, a hidden spark.

Roses bloom in barren ground,
Echoes of laughter, a muted sound.
Shattered dreams with wings still soar,
A paradox that asks for more.

Hope entwined with threads of despair,
Beauty found in the stark bare air.
Life's canvas painted with blurs and strokes,
Each contradiction softly provokes.

Embrace the chaos, hold it tight,
In every shadow, there's a light.
A dance of opposing, a tender fight,
On this canvas, contradictions ignite.

Unveiling the Unseen

Behind the veil where secrets hide,
Layers of truth begin to bide.
Whispers linger, softly seep,
Awakening wonders buried deep.

Silent stories, shadows cast,
Flickers of moments, gone too fast.
Eyes closed tight, yet vision clear,
In the invisible, dreams draw near.

Threads of fate, intricate lace,
Hopes entwined in time and space.
Beneath the surface, a pulse beats strong,
Unveiling the unseen, where we belong.

Let the light shine through the cracks,
Discover the whispers, follow the tracks.
In layers revealed, we find our grace,
A world transformed, a sacred place.

The Balance of a Feather

In gentle flight, a feather drifts,
Carried softly on nature's lifts.
Weightless dreams, a delicate dance,
Life's fragility in a fleeting chance.

Balanced on breezes, it sways and turns,
The heart's desires, the fire that burns.
In stillness found, in motion too,
With every flutter, the world feels new.

A symbol of peace, of freedom's call,
In its lightness, we rise, we fall.
The dance of life, a tender tether,
All exists in the balance of a feather.

As winds can shift, so can our fate,
What we hold dear we contemplate.
In every heartbeat, in even small tether,
Life's equilibrium rests, like a feather.

Poems from the Inbetween

In the hush of moments, where silence speaks,
Lies the inbetween, where the heart seeks.
Half-formed thoughts, shadows of grace,
In each lingering pause, we find our place.

Between the tick and the gentle tock,
In every heartbeat, a timeless clock.
Words left unsaid, connections shy,
In the gap of breaths, our spirits fly.

Echoes of laughter, remnants of tears,
The inbetween cradles hopes and fears.
In fleeting glances, in whispers low,
A sanctuary where our dreams can grow.

So here's to the inbetween, our quiet song,
Where fragments of life blend right and wrong.
In every crevice, we weave and spin,
A tapestry of poems from the inbetween.

When Hope Meets Hesitation

In shadows where dreams dare to tread,
A flicker of light, a thread of dread.
Whispers of courage, the heart's gentle plea,
Yet doubts in the silence, they cling like a sea.

As dawn breaks anew, bright visions take flight,
Yet fear coils around, a thief in the night.
Between the two worlds, a struggle unfolds,
Hope's fragile wings brushed with hesitation's cold.

In moments of stillness, decisions collide,
Each choice a path where emotions reside.
With every heartbeat, the tension will rise,
As hope reaches out, hesitation replies.

Yet through the confusion, a spark may ignite,
To dance with the shadows, to embrace the fight.
For when hope stands tall, and fear fades away,
A new dawn will blossom, brightening the day.

Journey Through a Conflicted Heart

In valleys of longing, I wander alone,
Chasing reflections that call me back home.
My heart like a compass, both lost and unsure,
Each beat is a question, is love ever pure?

Mountains of memories rise high in the mist,
Every peak bears witness to moments I've kissed.
Yet rivers of sorrow carve deep in my soul,
Drawing maps of my dreams, where kindness was whole.

I stand at the crossroads, with choices to make,
The whispers of passion and reason awake.
Which path leads to solace, which veers into night,
When shadows of doubt take away all my light?

Yet in all the chaos, a truth will emerge,
That love is a journey, forever to surge.
With every heart's conflict, a lesson unfolds,
In the depths of the struggle, pure beauty beholds.

A Song of Opposites

In twilight's embrace, day battles the night,
Where shadows and colors collide in their fight.
Each star tells a story of dreams set adrift,
As silence and chaos exchange a swift gift.

In laughter, there lingers a hint of the pain,
The sun greets the rain, a sweet bitter strain.
Joy dances with sorrow in delicate spins,
A melody woven from losses and wins.

The mountains stand tall, yet valleys run deep,
In beauty's reflection, the heart starts to weep.
With every soft whisper and every loud shout,
A song of opposites, casting shadows about.

For life is a tapestry, tangled yet bright,
Intermixed with the darkness and woven with light.
In harmony's clash, we find balance and grace,
A song of existence, a beautiful place.

Veils of Complexity

In layers of fabric, truths twist and entwine,
Each thread tells a story, both yours and mine.
Beneath the soft surface, reflections lie thin,
As shadows of longing weave chaos within.

The world wears its masks, a delicate guise,
Where laughter can echo, while sorrow can rise.
Yet in every silence, a heartbeat will swell,
In the depths of complexity, secrets may dwell.

With every new dawn, the patterns evolve,
The heart seeks the answers that time can't resolve.
Amidst all the noise, the soul learns to speak,
A whisper of truth found in moments unique.

And so through the veils that shroud every thought,
We navigate spaces where love is still sought.
In searches for meaning, we forge and we break,
Embracing the layers, our spirit awake.

Spirals of Uncertainty

In the midst of endless turns,
Questions hover, brightly burn.
Paths unseen, whispers call,
Wandering souls in the thrall.

Time unwinds like flowing thread,
Fears and hopes, both tangled, spread.
Each choice made, a winding fate,
Left to chance, or sealed by state.

Amidst the fog, we test and learn,
Facing shadows, hearts still yearn.
In the spiral, we find our way,
Guided softly, come what may.

Symphonies of Sorrow and Joy

Melodies play in shadows dim,
Notes of laughter, soft and grim.
Joy and sorrow, intertwined,
Echoes of what love designed.

Strings that resonate with pain,
Harmony beneath the rain.
In the silence, a heartbeat's plea,
Finding peace in symphony.

Crescendo builds, emotions soar,
Life's grand tale, forevermore.
Gathered close, we sway and blend,
In this song, may we transcend.

Claustrophobic Cosmos

Stars are trapped in velvet night,
Bound by dreams, yet seeking flight.
Galaxies whisper secrets tight,
In the depths, an aching light.

Atoms dance in crowded space,
Silent screams, a hurried pace.
Within these walls, we search for breath,
Feel the weight of unseen death.

Vast the void, yet we feel small,
Yearning to break that cosmic wall.
In the stillness, echoes roam,
Waiting to find a way back home.

Inner Dialogues and Dissonance

Voices clash within my mind,
Wrestling thoughts, each shift, unkind.
Truth and doubt, an endless fight,
Seeking calm in restless night.

Reflections caught in fractured glass,
Every moment lost, we pass.
Whispers rise, like ghostly flames,
Fragmented hope, forgotten names.

Yet in silence, clarity shines,
Through the chaos, wisdom finds.
Embrace the noise, let it flow,
In dissonance, we learn to grow.

In the Quiet of Tumultuous Hearts

Amidst the storm, we find our peace,
A gentle place where sorrows cease.
In shadows cast by restless fears,
Love's whisper calms the loudest tears.

Silent battles rage within,
Yet hearts entwined, defy the din.
With every breath, we mend the fray,
In quiet moments, we find our way.

Voices tremble, secrets shared,
In stillness found, we know we're cared.
Through tempest winds, our souls will soar,
Together strong, forevermore.

In tumult's heart, we find our song,
A melody where we belong.
In the chaos, true love's part,
In the quiet of tumultuous hearts.

The Hidden Depths of Contentment

In the stillness of a summer's night,
Contentment blooms, a gentle light.
Each simple joy, a treasure rare,
Found in moments, hearts laid bare.

Beneath the surface, peace resides,
In laughter shared and love that guides.
The world may rush, in haste it moves,
Yet in stillness, our spirit groves.

From whispered thoughts to dreams unfurled,
The hidden depths of our small world.
In every glance, a warmth is found,
Contentment's grace in soft surround.

Though chaos reigns beyond our door,
Within our hearts, we cherish more.
In quiet spaces, souls convene,
The hidden depths where we are seen.

Whispers in the Void

Between the stars, a silence reigns,
Echoes lost in endless plains.
Yet every star, a tale to tell,
In whispers soft, do secrets dwell.

In the void, where shadows play,
A distant light, the heart's array.
Feel the pull of cosmic grace,
In the vastness, find our place.

Voices linger, faint but clear,
In the darkness, draw them near.
For even voids have songs to sing,
In every absence, hope takes wing.

Beneath the quiet, truths abide,
In whispers soft, dreams coincide.
The vast unknown, a canvas wide,
With whispers in the void, we glide.

A Dance of Dilemmas

In the shadow of choices, we sway,
A dance of dilemmas, night and day.
Do we follow the heart or the mind?
In tangled steps, what will we find?

Every turn, a question bold,
A story in every choice retold.
In the rhythm of doubt, we advance,
Finding promise in this dance.

With every misstep, wisdom grows,
In the waltz of life, our path we chose.
Through turns and twists, we learn to see,
In this dance of dilemmas, we are free.

The music swells, the lights dim low,
With every heartbeat, our spirits flow.
And in this whirl, let's not forget,
In the dance of dilemmas, we're not done yet.

The Beauty in the Confusion

In chaos blooms a vibrant hue,
A dance of thoughts, both old and new.
Lost in the fog yet finding light,
In tangled paths, we take our flight.

The whispers blend, a gentle song,
In every note, we find where we belong.
Colors swirl in every shade,
In confusion, beauty is laid.

Fragments of dreams upon the floor,
In disarray, we search for more.
Among the noise, a heartbeat thuds,
A symphony of life's great floods.

So let us weave this tapestry,
Of joy and sorrow, wild and free.
In messy threads, life's art is true,
The beauty lies in all we do.

Intricate Web of Emotion

Threads of joy and strands of pain,
We weave them close, we let them wane.
In the shadows, feelings creep,
In the silence, secrets keep.

A tapestry of heart and mind,
Each stitch a moment intertwined.
The delicate dance of push and pull,
In every tear, our hearts are full.

We navigate this tender maze,
With gentle hands, we seek the praise.
For in the twists, our truths unfold,
A story rich, a heart of gold.

Amidst the chaos, we find our thread,
Each emotion spoken, each word unsaid.
A world alive with vibrant hues,
An intricate web, forever true.

The Stillness of a Swirling Mind

In a tempest's eye, there's calm to find,
The whispers of the swirling mind.
Thoughts collide like waves at sea,
Yet stillness holds a place for me.

In every swirl, a chance to see,
The beauty of uncertainty.
Amidst the chaos, peace appears,
In silent moments, we confront our fears.

The storm may rage, but deep inside,
A quiet truth begins to guide.
Through shifting sands of endless thought,
A tranquil heart is slowly sought.

So breathe the stillness, let it flow,
In every whirl, let wisdom grow.
A dialogue of soul and time,
The stillness sings, the heart's sweet rhyme.

Wading Through Waters of Ambivalence

Knee-deep in doubts, I stand and stare,
In murky waters, I'm stripped bare.
Choices ripple like the passing tide,
In indecision, truths collide.

The currents pull, I feel the sway,
In thoughts at odds, I lose my way.
A foot in one, a foot in both,
Caught between the circles of growth.

With heavy hearts, we wade anew,
In waters deep, we seek what's true.
But every splash reveals a taste,
Of freedom found amidst the haste.

Through these waters, I'll learn to flow,
Embrace the depths, let courage grow.
In ambivalence, my spirit sings,
The beauty in the choice it brings.

Echoes of Contemplative Dilemmas

In shadows deep where thoughts collide,
A maze of choices, we must abide.
Each path a whisper, a fork in time,
The mind a echo, a silent chime.

Caught in the web of dreams and fears,
Counting the days through silent tears.
What call we heed, what fate we choose?
In this dilemma, who stands to lose?

Voices of reason blend with the haze,
Mapping our lives through a nebulous maze.
We falter and stumble, yet stand tall,
In the echo of choices, we rise or fall.

Yet wisdom waits in the wings to speak,
Through quiet moments, it finds the meek.
As echoes linger, we find our way,
In contemplative silence, we learn to sway.

Reflections in a Shattered Mirror

Fragments glinting in the dim light,
Truths scattered, lost in the night.
Each piece a story, a tale once bright,
Now blurred memories take flight.

Faces familiar, yet twisted and strange,
Time's cruel hand has wrought the change.
Once whole and clear, a self-defined,
Now splintered visions claw at the mind.

In cracks and fissures, hope may shine,
A glimmer, a glimpse, a tender line.
Yet every shard holds a hidden pain,
In the broken image, we seek to gain.

We piece together with trembling hands,
Searching for meaning in shifting sands.
In shattered mirrors, reflections call,
To confront the darkness, to rise, not fall.

Whispers of the Unsaid

In quiet corners, secrets reside,
Silent echoes where truths confide.
Words left unspoken, heavy they lay,
Yearning to break through the veil of gray.

Softly they linger, like shadows at noon,
A melody played to a silent tune.
Fears intertwine with hopes tucked away,
In whispers of longing, we drift and sway.

Conversations held in a tender gaze,
Unraveling thoughts through a wistful haze.
What can't be voiced often roams free,
In the space of 'us', the unspoken plea.

Yet still we gather these whispers so dear,
For in the unspoken, the heart draws near.
Among the murmurs of truth we seek,
In silence, we find what words cannot speak.

The Contradiction of Silent Screams

A cry within, yet silence reigns,
A battle fought in hidden chains.
The heart beats loud, but lips stay sealed,
In the contradiction, we find what's revealed.

Screams echo softly, unheard by the world,
Within them, stories of pain unfurled.
Eyes may shimmer, yet voices decay,
In silent screams, we learn to sway.

Each moment stretches, a test of grace,
In the absence of sound, we search for a place.
What struggles to surface must twist and turn,
In the depths of silence, our passions burn.

Yet deep in the quiet, strength is born,
Emerging phoenix, from pain is torn.
In silent screams, resilience gleams,
A testament to life, to shattered dreams.

Fractal Thoughts in a Distant World

In shadows cast by fractured light,
Ideas bloom, surreal and bright.
Echoes swirl in cosmic streams,
Each thought a whisper, woven dreams.

Patterns rise and fade away,
Infinite in their quiet play.
Between the nodes, a spark ignites,
Fractal truths in endless flights.

From depths of void to skies' embrace,
A dance of minds in timeless space.
Each twist reveals a hidden core,
A world alive to explore.

In distant realms, the fractals swirl,
A universe, a boundless pearl.
Connecting threads of mystic signs,
In fractal thoughts, our fate aligns.

To Love an Uncertainty

In twilight's glow, we find our place,
Between the heartbeats, a soft grace.
Love dances near the edge of doubt,
In shadows deep, our dreams shout out.

Each glance a tether, fragile, true,
A quiet spark amidst the blue.
To love the unknown, boldly we tread,
In whispered fears, our feelings spread.

Moments hang like stars in night,
Unraveled truths in borrowed light.
In tender chaos, we breathe as one,
Two souls entwined, 'neath the same sun.

We embrace the storm, the calm, the change,
In every twist, we find what's strange.
To love an uncertainty, we dare,
In every heartbeat, we lay bare.

The Dance of Contrasts

In twilight's hues, the colors clash,
Light and darkness, a vivid flash.
Joy intertwined with shades of pain,
In every loss, a chance to gain.

Whispers soft and echoes bold,
Warmth and chill, the stories told.
Life's grand tapestry weaves and bends,
In sharp relief, where vision lends.

Silent nights, the raucous days,
In every moment, a thousand ways.
To cherish peace, we seek out strife,
In duality, we find our life.

The dance of contrasts, wild and free,
A canvas brushed with endless glee.
From shadows deep, our colors rise,
In the heart's embrace, love never lies.

Intersecting Lines of Fate

Two paths converge, a fleeting glance,
In swirling winds, we take a chance.
Life's intricate web, a fateful thread,
Lines intertwine where angels tread.

Moments pause, in silent grace,
As destiny draws near our space.
Each choice a marker on time's wide road,
A story written in each abode.

Across the miles, our spirits call,
In every rise, there lies a fall.
Like rivers meet, our fates entwine,
In the heart's mural, stars align.

Into the unknown, we brightly step,
With every breath, a promise kept.
The journey flows, a dance embraced,
In intersecting lines, love is traced.

Between Light and Shadow's Embrace

In twilight's gentle sigh, we stand,
Where whispers weave the day,
The dance of dusk, a soft command,
As dreams begin to sway.

The sun dips low, a painted brush,
On edges of the night,
In silence, hear the heart's deep hush,
Between dark and light.

Stars twinkle like forgotten lore,
In absence of the sun,
The mingling of what was before,
In shadows, we are one.

So let us linger in this phase,
Where moments softly blend,
In light and shadow's tender gaze,
A journey without end.

The Duality of Serenity

In whispers of the morning breeze,
A calm that fills the air,
Yet storms can brew beneath the trees,
Contradictions everywhere.

The stillness hides a vibrant heart,
A softness, yet a fire,
Each element plays its own part,
In a dance that does inspire.

With every breath, a sacred calm,
A balance we must find,
For even in the fiercest storm,
There lies a peace enshrined.

Embrace the chaos, hold it tight,
For in the clash of fate,
We find the beauty of the light,
In every twist of state.

Threads of Unraveled Thoughts

Woven in the mind's own maze,
Loose threads begin to show,
A tapestry of fleeting days,
In patterns ebb and flow.

Each stitch a memory held dear,
Each knot a tangled fight,
In quiet hours, the truth draws near,
Illuminated light.

We gather fragments of our dreams,
And weave them strong and tight,
In hopes that from the frayed extremes,
A vision finds its sight.

So let us unearth these lost strands,
Reconnect the faded lore,
With gentle hearts and open hands,
We'll write our story more.

Beneath the Surface of Still Waters

A mirror holds the sky's embrace,
In quiet ripples, sighs,
Beneath the calm, a hidden place,
Where truth and mystery lies.

The depths conceal, yet softly speak,
Of currents strong and deep,
In silence, wisdom finds the meek,
Awakens from its sleep.

As shadows dance on liquid glass,
The world above is bright,
Yet down below, the moments pass,
In whispers of the night.

To dive into the waters clear,
Is to uncover grace,
For every fear that once was near,
Finds strength in this embrace.

Navigating Shadows of the Self

In the mirror, fragments gleam,
Unsure of what they truly mean.
Whispers dance in silent night,
Chasing echoes, seeking light.

Steps through fog, a wraith-like trace,
Lost within this hidden space.
Yet in the dark, a spark ignites,
Guiding hearts to higher flights.

Threads of fear, a tangled thread,
Fears we carry, heavy dread.
But through each shadow, truth will show,
The light within will learn to glow.

Finding strength in gentle grace,
Each step forward, a new embrace.
In the silence, spirits call,
To navigate, we rise and fall.

Between the Lines of a Dream

Where whispers weave, a tale unfolds,
Lost in the twilight, beauty holds.
Images dance, softly they glide,
Between the lines where hopes reside.

In silver mist, thoughts take flight,
Chasing shadows, fading light.
A heartbeat lingers, time drifts away,
In the stillness, dreams learn to play.

Through vibrant hues, stories collide,
Of wanderers who dare to confide.
In realms unseen, our spirits soar,
Between the lines, we seek for more.

Awakened hearts, free to explore,
Through hidden paths and timeless lore.
Between the dreams, where souls unite,
We find our wings, take fearless flight.

The Enigma of Now

In the stillness, time stands clear,
Moments whisper, close and near.
Each heartbeat a secret song,
An enigma where we belong.

Caught in the pulse of life's embrace,
The here and now, a sacred space.
Questions linger in the air,
Wrapped in wonder, pulling care.

Through tangled thoughts, clarity peeks,
In subtle glances, silence speaks.
A breath, a pause, the world slows down,
In the chaos, peace is found.

The dance of time, both cruel and kind,
Chasing moments that bind.
In the enigma, we shall see,
The beauty in simply being free.

Chasing Illusions Beneath the Stars

Under a shroud of velvet night,
Stars cascade, a wondrous sight.
Whispers of dreams drift on the breeze,
Chasing hopes, like dancing leaves.

Nebulae bright, a cosmic trace,
Illusions flicker in boundless space.
With every wish cast to the sky,
We search for truth where shadows lie.

Each glimmer holds a tale untold,
Of love, of pain, both fierce and bold.
In the silence, secrets bloom,
Beneath the stars, we find our room.

Yet in the vastness, fears reside,
As we navigate this endless tide.
Chasing illusions, still we stand,
In the night's embrace, hand in hand.

Where Certainty Meets Ambiguity

In shadows cast by doubt's embrace,
Two paths converge, time cannot trace.
One whispers truth, the other lies,
In this limbo, the spirit flies.

Clarity fades like morning mist,
Certainties fade, dreams persist.
A dance on lines both light and dark,
Where hope ignites its vivid spark.

Each choice a thread, a tapestry spun,
Weaving stories 'til day is done.
Amidst the chaos, find your way,
In shades of gray, let spirit sway.

The heart seeks solace, yet yearns to roam,
In ambiguity, we find our home.
Where certainty dims under night's deep dome,
Life's exquisite ambiguity, our poem.

A Symphony of Unrelated Notes

Fingers dance on ivory keys,
Unscripted sounds ride the breeze.
A clash of rhythms, wild and free,
In this chaos, we find harmony.

Melodies intertwine like vines,
Each note unique, yet it aligns.
In discord, a beauty shines bright,
A symphony painted in colors of light.

Whispers of joy, shouts of despair,
Notes collide in the cool night air.
From silence emerges a soul's release,
In a world of noise, there lies peace.

Together in chaos, we stand unafraid,
A symphony born from the choices made.
In unrelated notes, life finds its song,
A melody shared, where we all belong.

The Fragility of a Fading Dream

Once vibrant hues, now pale and thin,
A flicker of light held deep within.
Whispers of hope, soft as a sigh,
As echoes linger, they slowly die.

Fragile threads weave stories lost,
In a journey bound by hidden cost.
Memory dances, a ghostly gleam,
Chasing shadows of a fading dream.

Yet in the twilight, new sparks ignite,
Through scattered ashes, we find our light.
In every ending, a chance reborn,
The fragile heart wakes with each dawn.

Though dreams may fade like mist in flight,
They shape our souls, fierce and bright.
In the stillness, embrace what seems,
For life's own fabric is stitched with dreams.

Embracing the Storm Within

Thunder rumbles, whispers grow,
A tempest brews where few dare go.
Yet in the chaos, strength ignites,
Holding tight through wild flights.

Winds of change, fierce and bold,
Unravel truths that once were told.
In darker skies, find your song,
For in the storm, we all belong.

Lightning dances, shadows shift,
From inner turmoil, new gifts lift.
Embrace the storm, let it unfurl,
As calmness stirs in a swirling whirl.

Through every gale, a lesson learned,
In the fire of passion, the spirit burned.
With each tempest, rise and spin,
To embrace the storm, and thrive within.

Reflections on a Twilit Mind

In twilight's grasp, thoughts softly dance,
A fleeting glance, a whispered chance.
Shadows merge, the day meets night,
In quietude, we find the light.

Mirrors show what we conceal,
A world of dreams that seem so real.
In every echo, secrets twine,
The mind reveals what hearts define.

Fragments of a world obscure,
A maze of thoughts we must endure.
Yet in the dark, reflections gleam,
A tapestry of hope and dream.

As night unfolds, we start to see,
The light within, setting it free.
In twilight's calm, we find our way,
To the dawn of a brand new day.

The Heart's Contradiction

Between desire and fear, we sway,
A constant tug, night and day.
Love ignites yet numbs the soul,
A bitter fight for lasting goal.

In joy we find the tinge of pain,
A laughing heart, yet hush of rain.
To trust is to open, to yield,
Yet in that openness, we shield.

What feels so right can turn so wrong,
A whispered shame inside our song.
In paradox, we bloom and fade,
A tapestry of dreams we've laid.

Yet still we love, despite the cost,
Embracing every gain and loss.
In contradictions, we are whole,
The heart's sweet ache, a restless goal.

Shadows of Uncertainty

In the hush of dusk, doubts unfold,
A tale of whispers, both meek and bold.
Paths diverge in the fading light,
A dance with shadows that stirs the night.

Questions linger in silent air,
What we seek, we cannot bear.
In every choice, a price to pay,
A constant pull between the gray.

The fear of loss, it holds us tight,
Yet in that grip, we find our fight.
For shadows teach what light can't show,
In uncertainty, we learn to grow.

Embrace the doubt, let it reside,
For in confusion, wisdom hides.
With every breath, we take the leap,
Into the depths, our souls to keep.

Tangled Threads of Thought

In a web of dreams, we find our way,
Tangled threads lead us astray.
Each notion pulls, entwined in fate,
A puzzle formed we seek to mate.

Whispers swirl like autumn leaves,
Caught in currents that rarely cleave.
Ideas clash, yet some align,
In chaos lies a hidden sign.

Through winding paths, we navigate,
Seeking clarity, we contemplate.
For in the fray, connections spark,
Illuminating the hidden dark.

Perhaps the mess is worth the strife,
A tapestry of thoughts in life.
With each embrace of tangled thread,
We weave the stories left unsaid.

Fragmented Realities

In shards of glass, the world appears,
Reflections dance through silent tears.
Colors bleed, the edges fray,
Lost in thought, we drift away.

A tapestry of hope and dread,
Woven threads of words unsaid.
Voices whisper, shadows play,
Fragmented dreams in disarray.

Time unravels, moments blend,
Each heartbeat a means to an end.
Caught in loops of fleeting time,
We chase the echoes, lost in rhyme.

Yet in the void, there lies a spark,
A flicker bright against the dark.
In pieces we find who we are,
Fragments unite, a guiding star.

Unfolding Mask of Duality

Behind the smile, a shadow lurks,
A hidden truth that often works.
In laughter's echo, silence sighs,
Two worlds collide beneath the skies.

The mask we wear, a shield of grace,
Hides the turmoil, the inner chase.
In every heartbeat, joy and pain,
The weather shifts, the heart's terrain.

In moments bright, the shadows creep,
Awakening dreams we long to keep.
Yet here we stand, both night and day,
Unfolding layers in disarray.

To be whole, we must embrace,
The light and dark, the endless space.
In this dance of duality,
We find the truth, our reality.

Between Light and Shade

In twilight's glow, the world does pause,
A dance of shadows, nature's laws.
Soft whispers blend, then fade away,
Caught in the realm of light and shade.

The sun dips low, a golden hue,
While stars awaken, one by one, too.
A canvas painted with dusk's embrace,
Where dreams unfold in timeless space.

In every shadow, a story lives,
The secrets that the silence gives.
Between the beams, a mystery,
The balance found in symmetry.

So let us wander, hand in hand,
Between the light, through shadowed land.
In this liminal, we shall find,
The beauty held, both heart and mind.

The Riddle of Reflection

In mirrors, truths come dressed in guise,
With every glance, a new surprise.
We ponder deep what lies within,
The riddle spun, where dreams begin.

Echoes linger in the glass,
Past and present, moments pass.
What do we seek in every stare?
The hidden layers, the heart laid bare.

Questions swirl like autumn leaves,
Seeking answers as the heart believes.
In every image, thoughts collide,
The depth of self, our inner guide.

To understand this fleeting game,
We must confront the shifting frame.
For in reflection, life's revealed,
The riddle shared, a truth unsealed.

The Art of Unanswered Questions

In silent whispers echoes call,
The mind debates, a constant brawl.
Each thought a bird that dares to fly,
Yet holds its truth beneath the sky.

Questions linger, shadows dance,
In every glance, a hidden chance.
The heart and mind, a tangled thread,
Seeking answers where none are bred.

A puzzle piece without a mate,
We ponder time, we question fate.
The art resides in thoughts unspun,
Where every answer's just begun.

With every doubt, a path appears,
We learn to wade through hopes and fears.
The beauty lies in not knowing,
In the questions, life's seeds are growing.

Lost in the Labyrinth of Introspection

Within the maze, I walk alone,
Each turn, a chance to find my own.
Reflections mute, but voices loud,
In silence wrapped, I feel the shroud.

Walls of thought, they twist and blend,
A labyrinth where shadows bend.
Each step a search for hidden light,
In corridors of endless night.

Memories echo with each sigh,
Fragments linger, asking why.
Questions spiral, truths evade,
In this mind's maze, I am delayed.

Yet in the depths, a spark ignites,
A courage found through endless flights.
In twists and turns, I seek the way,
To find the dawn within the grey.

The Balance of Fragile Fortitude

In delicate strength, I find my ground,
A whispering will, a quiet sound.
The battles fought within my heart,
Where courage blooms, but doubts depart.

I stand on cliffs of shifting sand,
With visions clear, yet trembling hand.
A fortress built from fragile dreams,
In valleys deep, the sunlight beams.

Resilience rests in quiet grace,
In every scar, a soft embrace.
A balance swings between the two,
Fragile heart and spirit true.

Each falter, every rise and fall,
Teaches me to hear the call.
In strength's embrace, I learn to be,
A beacon shining, wild and free.

Poems of Inward Struggles

Within the soul, a storm does brew,
Each tempest fierce, bringing the blue.
Words left unspoken, heavy weight,
In the depths, I contemplate fate.

The mirror reflects a troubled gaze,
In shadows cast, I spend my days.
A battle waged beneath the skin,
Inward wars where few have been.

Through tangled thoughts, I weave each line,
In poems penned, my truths entwined.
Elegy for what I can't say,
Inward struggles find their way.

Yet with each verse, a light breaks free,
A gentle nudge to simply be.
Through written words, I start to heal,
In every line, the heart's appeal.

The Silence of a Thousand Voices

In shadows deep, where whispers dwell,
A quiet sigh begins to swell.
The echoes fade, the moments lost,
Yet still we search, despite the cost.

Through tangled webs of thoughts confined,
A thousand dreams are left behind.
In stillness, we find truths restrained,
The silent cries of hopes unnamed.

Each voice a thread, in silence spun,
A tapestry of dreams undone.
We hold them close, though faint they seem,
In silence, they weave through our dream.

For in that hush, the heart can hear,
The depth of pain, the edge of fear.
A chorus found in quiet's grace,
The silence holds a sacred space.

Waves of Uncertainty

Upon the shore, the tides do rise,
A dance of doubt beneath the skies.
Each wave that crashes brings a chance,
To sink or swim in fate's great dance.

The ocean churns with restless cues,
In depths unknown, we seek the hues.
A current pulls, uncertainty reigns,
Yet still we sail through joy and pains.

The horizon shifts, the wind does change,
A compass lost, it feels so strange.
But in the ebb, a lesson learned,
The heart finds strength, as tides are turned.

We ride the waves, through storm and calm,
In uncertainty, we find the balm.
For every crest, a fall brings light,
In the dance of doubt, we find our might.

A Heart Divided by Choice

Two paths before me stretch ahead,
With each step, I weigh the dread.
One whispers soft, the other loud,
In silence cloaked, and in the crowd.

A heart once whole now feels the strain,
With hopes and dreams wrapped in the chain.
Each choice a thread, a line that's drawn,
In twilight's glow, I greet the dawn.

What if I choose the road less known?
Or take the path where seeds are sown?
In restless nights, I search for peace,
Yet in the divide, my doubts increase.

A heart torn wide, can love endure?
In choices bound, the soul's unsure.
But through the struggle, I will find,
The strength to live, the choice to bind.

Revelations from the Abyss

In depths profound, the shadows creep,
Where secrets lie and silence weeps.
A journey dark, yet voices call,
To pierce the heart, to break the fall.

Each revelation, like a spark,
Illuminates the hidden dark.
In whispers soft, the truth unfolds,
In every story, courage molds.

From depths unknown, the light shall rise,
To greet the dawn and clear the skies.
For in the abyss, we truly see,
The strength within, to set us free.

So dive into the darkened sea,
Embrace the truth and let it be.
The revelations call us forth,
From depths of pain, to new-found worth.

The Fragile Balance

A whisper in the breeze, so light,
Feathers floating, taking flight.
Beneath the surface, tensions grow,
Holding strong, yet slipping low.

The sun sets fast, the shadows creep,
Promises promised, secrets keep.
In dreams we wander, lost and found,
In fragile balance, we are bound.

Each heartbeat counts, a fragile thread,
Moments cherished, words left said.
The scale tips gently, sides aligned,
In every choice, a truth confined.

Yet here we stand, on shifting ground,
With every heartbeat, we are crowned.
In harmony, our spirits dance,
Embracing life, we take the chance.

Surrendering to Unknowing

In depths of night, we close our eyes,
Letting go of all the ties.
The future waits, both bright and dim,
A tapestry of hope and whim.

Waves of doubt crash on the shore,
Yet in stillness, we seek more.
With hands wide open, hearts awake,
We step beyond, for love's own sake.

In every question, life unfolds,
A story waiting to be told.
We dance on edges of the unknown,
Surrendering to seeds we've sown.

With every breath, the fear subsides,
In shadows linger, truth abides.
Embrace the chaos, let it flow,
Surrendering to what we don't know.

Labyrinth of Longing

In winding paths of heart's desire,
Whispers echo, dreams conspire.
A maze of longing, twists and turns,
In every corner, passion burns.

Footsteps falter, doubts take flight,
Searching in the dead of night.
Through tangled thoughts, we chase the light,
In labyrinth of love's sweet plight.

Every turn reveals a sigh,
A flicker of what might comply.
The heart, relentless, seeks its way,
Through shadows cast by yesterday.

Yet in the chaos, beauty gleams,
Amid the doubt, we chase our dreams.
A labyrinth where we must stray,
In longing's grip, we choose to stay.

Inkwells of Inconsistency

With every stroke, the ink may blur,
A thought obscured, a silent stir.
Inkwells hold the tales untold,
Of laughter warm and hearts gone cold.

Moments shift like grains of sand,
Certainty slips from our hand.
Yet through the chaos, words arise,
In every truth, a hidden guise.

A canvas blank, a writer's plight,
Where shadows play in morning light.
Inconsistent lines, yet still we dare,
To pour our souls, a story bare.

So let the ink flow on the page,
In vulnerability, we engage.
For even in the haze we find,
Inconsistency can be quite kind.

Where Dreams and Reality Collide

In twilight's haze, shadows blend,
Where whispers of hope and fears suspend.
Stars flicker bright, like secrets untold,
As the heart dares to dream, both timid and bold.

A canvas painted with hues of the night,
Waves of emotions crash, taking flight.
Reality's grip begins to unwind,
As visions take shape, both gentle and blind.

Through tangled paths, we wander alone,
Dancing on lines of the known and unknown.
In the space between breaths, magic is found,
Where dreams and reality spin round and round.

The echoes of laughter, the sighs of the air,
Moments of solace, light as a prayer.
A bridge stretching far, to the depths of the soul,
Where dreams and reality unite, becoming whole.

The Fragility of Balance

On a beam of trust, we often tread,
In a dance of chaos, where doubts are fed.
A waltz with shadows, a partner in plight,
The fragile balance of day and night.

With every step, the ground may quake,
Yet in the stillness, the heart may awake.
Holding the weight of the world in our hands,
A fleeting moment, like slipping sands.

Between joy and sorrow, we strive to align,
In the delicate weave of fate's subtle design.
A heartbeat echoes, a silent plea,
In this fragile balance, we yearn to be free.

With courage, we face the storms that arise,
In the mirror of life, we see our own eyes.
A fleeting breath, yet we stand tall,
Embracing the beauty, embracing the fall.

Cracks in a Perfect Illusion

A mask of joy hides the tears within,
In the guise of perfection, where flaws begin.
Shattered reflections dance on the wall,
Echoes of truth in a grand masquerade ball.

Underneath layers of painted smiles,
Lie the fractures of life, spanning miles.
Each tiny crack tells a story untold,
Of hearts that have wandered, of dreams that are sold.

In search of solace, we drift and we sway,
Clinging to visions that fade day by day.
Yet the beauty lies in the story we weave,
In the cracks of illusion, we learn to believe.

As dawn breaks anew, hope starts to unfold,
In the light of acceptance, the brave and the bold.
Embracing our flaws, together we rise,
In the cracks of perfection, true beauty lies.

The Silence Between Questions

In the hush where thoughts collide,
Whispers of doubt linger wide.
Each pause a heavy breath held tight,
Finding truth in the absence of light.

Voices echo without a sound,
In the stillness, answers are found.
Questions float like autumn leaves,
Dancing softly in the mind's eaves.

What lies beyond the unasked words?
A world unseen, where silence curds.
Between the wants and needs, we tread,
In the quiet, fears gently spread.

Yet in this void, hope takes flight,
Casting shadows with fragile light.
For in the space where words don't flow,
The heart reveals what it longs to show.

Mirror of Conflicting Dreams

Underneath the surface glow,
Reflections twist, ebb, and flow.
Shattered visions, crystal clear,
In perfect chaos, truths appear.

A canvas painted with deep hues,
Dreams collide, each one a bruise.
What we wish and what we fear,
In the mirror, both draw near.

Whispers echo in violent dance,
Bound by fate, lost in a trance.
Each dream a story left untold,
In the glass, we seek the bold.

Chasing shadows of past desires,
We ignite our inner fires.
Yet in the clash, a spark remains,
A journey forged through joy and pains.

Echoes of Ambivalence

In twilight's glow, where feelings wane,
Ambivalence weaves a complex chain.
Torn between the push and pull,
In this space, hearts grow full.

Silent battles rage inside,
Each choice a wave upon a tide.
What to keep and what to flee,
Echoes linger, endlessly.

In the strength of the unsure,
Even doubt can find a cure.
To embrace what we cannot decide,
Is to let the heart confide.

Through the ambivalence, we learn,
In each twist, a chance to turn.
For in the echoes, life is spun,
In every shade, the light and sun.

Paradox Beneath the Surface

Beneath the calm, a storm resides,
In gentle waves, the chaos hides.
Truths intertwined in a tangled thread,
What's left unsaid is often read.

In still waters, secrets creep,
Awake the dreams we try to keep.
Yet contradictions lay the path,
To wisdom's fruit and folly's wrath.

In the shadows, clarity grows,
From the doubt, a river flows.
Embrace the duality we bear,
In every breath, a whispered prayer.

For within the paradox, we find,
A mirror to the wandering mind.
Where all is not as it appears,
Depths reveal both joy and fears.

When Truth Stumbles

In shadows deep, the truth does fade,
A whispered lie, in silence laid.
Footsteps falter, hearts entwined,
In shattered mirrors, we seek the blind.

The echo calls, a distant cry,
Where honesty once dared to fly.
Yet in the cracks, a glimpse remains,
A fleeting spark amidst the chains.

We chase the light through mist and fog,
While reason bows beneath the smog.
In tangled webs, our fates align,
As truth, once noble, starts to pine.

So let us dance this fragile waltz,
Embrace the flaws, accept our faults.
For truth, though stumbling, yearns to rise,
And find its home 'neath honest skies.

Reveries of the Reluctant

In quiet corners, dreams unfold,
Whispers of wishes, timid yet bold.
Minds wander slowly, paths unclear,
In shadows linger hopes and fear.

The heart hesitates, a fragile flame,
Yearning for warmth, yet bound by shame.
In reveries soft, the soul may glide,
But doubts like chains, they twist and chide.

Time ebbs like tides on distant shores,
Where fantasies linger, and longing soars.
Engagement wanes in fear's embrace,
As dreams retreat from time and space.

Yet still flickers the ember bright,
In the reluctant's silent fight.
For somewhere nestled within that strife,
May bloom the beauty of a new life.

Shattered Certainties

Once solid ground, now rifts and seams,
The world divided, unraveling dreams.
In vivid colors, chaos reigns,
While reason struggles against the chains.

What once was clear, now lost to doubt,
A game of chance, we dance about.
The weight of knowledge fades away,
As shadows stretch at end of day.

We clench our truths in trembling hands,
Yet nature laughs, as folly stands.
In questioned trust, we find despair,
Wandering souls, adrift in air.

But perhaps through shattered glass we see,
A tapestry woven, wild and free.
In broken pieces, art may thrive,
Reborn through chaos, we survive.

Embracing the Unfathomable

In depths unknown, where mysteries hide,
We seek the truth, though hearts may bide.
Stars above, they whisper low,
Secrets woven in cosmic flow.

The ocean's breath, a haunting call,
In waves of time, we rise and fall.
What fuels the fire of day's demise?
In shadows deep, the question lies.

With open arms, we face the night,
Unraveling dreams in silver light.
In every step toward the abyss,
We find the beauty in what we miss.

So let us roam where wisdom weeps,
In the unfathomable, the heart leaps.
For every moment, strange and grand,
Is a journey taken, hand in hand.

Milton Keynes UK
Ingram Content Group UK Ltd.
UKHW022117251124
451529UK00012B/579